Montreal
Botanical Garden

Text by Jean-Jacques Lincourt
in collaboration with Sylvie Perron

Translation by Glee Jessee Lauzière

Photographs by Louise Tanguay

FIDES

QUEBEC
GARDENS'
ASSOCIATION

Jean-Jacques Lincourt and Sylvie Perron would like to thank Stéphane M. Bailleul, Lucie Bossé, François Brousseau, Dave Demers, Normand Fleury, Brigitte Lefebvre, Madeleine Pronovost, and all of the horticulturists at the Montréal Botanical Garden for their contribution to this guide.

Louise Tanguay wishes to thank the Boréalis photographic laboratory for the quality of their work and their financial support.

The assistance of the ministère de l'Agriculture, des Pêcheries et de l'Alimentation, particularly the present minister, Maxime Arseneau, and his predecessor, Rémy Trudel, and their deputy-minister, Jacques Landry, has been essential in bringing to life this collection of guide books to Québec gardens.

For their dedication, which was instrumental in developing this project of celebrating Québec's horticultural heritage, thanks also go to Hélène Leclerc, directress of the Domaine Joly-De Lotbinière, and to Denis Messier of the Mackenzie-King Estate.

Graphic design: Gianni Caccia, Louise Tanguay
Cover: Louise Tanguay

Canadian Cataloguing in Publication Data
Lincourt, Jean-Jacques, 1955-
Montréal Botanical Garden
(Guides to the Gardens of Québec)
Translation of: Jardin botanique de Montréal
Includes bibliographical references and index.
ISBN 2-7621-2358-5

1. Montréal Botanical Garden. 2. Botanical Gardens – Québec (Province) –
Montréal. 3. Montréal Botanical Garden – Pictorial works.
I. Tanguay, Louise. II. Title. III. Series.

QK73.C32J37 2001a   580'.7'371428   C00-942319-2

Legal deposit: second quarter 2001
National Library of Québec
© Éditions Fides, 2001

The publisher wishes to thank the Canada Council for the Arts, the Department of Canadian Heritage, and the Société de développement des entreprises culturelles du Québec (SODEC) for their generous support of its publishing programs. The publisher is funded by the Government of Quebec tax credit program for publishing, a program managed by the SODEC.

Printed in Canada

Table of contents

Introduction

A we! In one word, that is the impression I got the first time I heard someone mention the Montréal Botanical Garden. I was seven years old and my mother was describing, with a multitude of flowery details, the trip she made with her sisters to the big city – Montréal – and more specifically their tour of the Botanical Garden. From that time on, I found myself dreaming of visiting this wonderful garden and exploring its innermost secrets.

It wasn't until a beautiful Sunday in the summer of 1962, as a young student registered in an ornamental horticulture program, that I was finally able to feel the impact of the feeling of wonderment that my mother and aunts had aroused in me.

I can still smell the fragrances of my first visit to the Montréal Botanical Garden. Having just received my diploma in horticulture, I could begin to imagine the expanse of the Garden and the richness of its vegetation, which only added to the delight I was feeling. That visit was a veritable revelation for me: the Garden offered such incredible potential and I could spend my entire life exploring it...

Today, some 25 years later, I continue my walks around the Garden at all hours of the day, every seasons of the year. Judging from the amount those walks have taught me and the plethora of emotions I still experience each time, I don't think I will ever grow tired of it. As I stroll around the Garden, I can't help thinking of the work done by my predecessors, the passion felt by the men and women who were the artisans of the Botanical Garden. They made it what it is today: a unique institution, renowned for its priceless

◁ *A flowering crabapple, floral emblem of the City of Montréal.*

◁ *Previous pages: floribunda roses.*

◁ *Korean azalea (Rhododendron yedoense var. poukhanense) in the Leslie Hancock Garden.*

▽ *The fall, in the Alpine Garden.*

collections, its educational mission, and its unfailing vitality.

I have an outstanding team working at the Garden, all driven by that same passion that has given life to the Garden since its beginnings, and that ensures its constant evolution. It is therefore with much enthusiasm and optimism that I look forward to taking on the new challenges that await the Garden at the beginning of this millennium.

It is my hope that this guide will make your experience at the Montréal Botanical Garden as enriching as the pleasure I have had in preparing it, and that you will get as much enjoyment as I as you walk along the paths and take in the beauty around you. The superb photographs by Louise Tanguay will enable you to recollect your most precious memories and your most enjoyable moments spent in this heaven on earth... Enjoy your visit!

Jean-Jacques Lincourt
Director, Montréal Botanical Garden

A BRIEF HISTORY

A Garden, a Passion

The history of the Montréal Botanical Garden is closely associated with one name: Brother Marie-Victorin, whose real name was Conrad Kirouac (1885-1944). Because of his political savvy and passion for science – a rare combination – he was finally able to convince the City of Montréal to build a large-scale botanical garden, and construction began in 1931.

The idea of providing the largest city in Québec with a botanical garden worthy of that name and capable of measuring up to the largest botanical gardens in the world, such as Kew Gardens in London or the *Jardin des plantes* in Paris, goes back to the middle of the 19th century. As early as 1863, others had tried to convince McGill University to sponsor the construction of such a garden in Montréal.

Twenty-two years later, in 1885, another project was put forward by a group that called itself the Montreal Botanical Garden Association. The plan was to build the garden on Mount Royal, but the project was aborted as a result of administrative problems with the City of Montréal.

It wasn't until the 1920s that the idea for a botanical garden came to a young botany professor, Brother Marie-Victorin.

The Garden Takes Shape

The first earth was finally turned over on the site of the Botanical Garden on May 7, 1936.

By 1939, the main parts of the Botanical Garden had been completed according to Henry Teuscher's drawings. Only the greenhouses still had to be built. The work had cost $11 million, a huge sum of money for the time. The Botanical Garden then consisted of an art deco administrative building adorned with fountains and waterfalls, and the formal gardens on the west side, which backed onto Boulevard Pie-IX.

Brother Marie-Victorin's Legacy

From the beginning, Marie-Victorin wanted the Garden to have an educational and scientific role. In 1938, the École d'apprentissage horticole (horticultural training school) was established and garden plots were set up for schoolchildren. The next year

▽ Pitcher plants (Sarracenia), Marie-Victorin's favourite flower.

△ The art deco administrative building in 1938.

△ Waterfalls in the Reception Gardens, in 1938.

▽ The first earth was turned over on May 7, 1936.

Brother Marie-Victorin

1885-1944

From the beginning of his career, Brother Marie-Victorin displayed a passion for science that was much ahead of his time in Québec. He carried out years of research that led to the publication of a book entitled *Flore laurentienne* (Laurentian flora). Even today, this remarkable work remains a reference book on the flora of Québec.

Marie-Victorin also conducted a botanical "laboratory" that would soon become the *Institut botanique pour le développement de l'enseignement et de la recherche universitaire* (botanical institute for the development of teaching and university research). In 1923, he founded ACFAS (a French-Canadian association for the advancement of science), a group that is still very active to this day. In 1925, he also became the executive secretary of the Natural History Society of Canada.

The artisan-founder of the Botanical Garden was not only an avid researcher. In order for his dream to become a reality, he also had to display great patience and be an excellent strategist, qualities that would enable him to carefully handle his political allies and his friends in the media.

The daily newspaper, *Le Devoir*, and politician Camilien Houde both gave the project their unfailing support over the years. The Garden was officially founded during Houde's first term as mayor of Montréal (1928-32). A small administration building and a service greenhouse were built, but Houde's defeat in 1932 and the Great Depression slowed down the difficult beginnings of the institution.

Three years later, in 1935, Houde was re-elected mayor of Montréal. Marie-Victorin sent him an impassioned plea in favour of the botanical garden, that was still really only in the planning stage.

"You need to give a gift, a royal gift, to the City, our city. But Montréal is Ville-Marie, a woman [...] and you certainly can't give her a storm sewer or a police station [...] It's obvious what you must do! Give her a corsage for her lapel. Fill her arms to overflowing with all the roses and lilies of the field."

Marie-Victorin didn't hesitate to use poetry as ammunition, for he hoped to take advantage of the fact that 1942 was the year that Montréal would celebrate its 300th anniversary.

Jacques Rousseau

Jacques Rousseau, a renowned botanist and explorer who had graduated from the *Institut botanique*, was the natural successor to the Garden's illustrious founder. He had drawn up a list of the various types of plants found in many regions of Québec, from Ungava Bay to the Saint Lawrence Valley. Loyal to Brother Marie-Victorin's ideas, Jacques Rousseau set about developing the Garden's scientific mission.

the *École de l'éveil* became part of the Garden. The purpose of this innovative institution was to provide young city dwellers with the opportunity to discover nature. In 1943, Marie-Victorin came up with a plan to create a formal association between the Garden and the *Institut botanique de l'Université de Montréal* (botanical institute of the University of Montréal), but his accidental death in the summer of 1944 put an end to that project.

The war years were difficult ones. All-around shortages meant rethinking priorities and postponing construction of the greenhouses. The Québec government was against spending money on that type of project. Then, if that wasn't enough, curator Henry Teuscher, who was originally from Germany, was falsely accused of spying for the Nazis. He would eventually be cleared, but the "Teuscher affair" was in the headlines for quite some time.

The exhibition greenhouses, an important part of Henry Teuscher's initial project, were finally built after the war. Jacques Rousseau was in charge of the construction work and Teuscher remained curator of the Garden.

The greenhouses were finally opened in 1956, just after the departure of Jacques Rousseau. Although the Botanical Garden experienced various problems – political rivalries and sometimes difficult relations with the *Institut botanique* – everyone involved with the Garden celebrated its 25th anniversary with a sense of accomplishment.

For the most part, Marie-Victorin and Henry Teuschers' project had become a reality. The Garden was true to its educational and scientific missions and the project had gained public interest. From the point of view of the diversity and significance of its collections, the Garden was a resounding success.

Conquering the World

The 1960s were not great years for the Garden and few new projects

Henry Teuscher, Designer of the Garden

Another of Marie-Victorin's valuable allies was Henry Teuscher. Initially a gardener at the Botanical Garden of Berlin, he later emigrated to the United States and acquired an excellent reputation as a horticulturist and landscape architect. He had held various posts relating to his field of specialization, one of which was dendrologist at the New York Botanical Garden. In the 1930s Teuscher began a long and productive correspondence with Marie-Victorin, who entrusted him with his project. Teuscher then set his imagination to work on plans for an ideal botanical garden. In spite of the distance separating them and political problems that were slowing down the realization of the project, the two men shared the same enthusiasm. Their alliance eventually led to Teuscher's being named curator of the new Montréal Botanical Garden.

▷ *The Youth Gardens, an activity that was started by Brother Marie-Victorin that is still hugely popular today.*

were undertaken. Henry Teuscher retired in 1962.

Development of the Garden took off again in the mid-1970s. Pierre Bourque became director in 1980. Scientific activities quickly resumed and world-wide interest in the Garden was sparked in the wake of the *Floralies internationales*, the highly successful international flower show held in the summer of 1980.

Renovation of the greenhouses, new equipment, increased collaboration with the University of Montréal, the creation of societies and associations, and the development of a professional ornamental horticulture training program are all examples of the Garden's impressive expansion during these years.

It was during this period that the Montréal Botanical Garden reached the level at which it is today: it ranks

among the largest botanical gardens in the world. The Japanese Garden was added, followed by the Chinese Garden, both remarkable successes. The Insectarium and the Tree House were added later.

True to its Mission

In 1990, officials at the City of Montréal and the University of Montréal agreed to create the Plant Biology Research Institute, which was substantially funded and equipped with a research team whose mandates involved both fundamental research and the transfer of technology.

As a result, there was a spectacular revival of the traditional scientific mission of the Garden, whose development had, admittedly, been rocky over the years. By the end of the 1990s, it was clear that scientific work carried out at the Botanical Garden was an inalienable component of its overall mission and a valuable tool in developing its national and international reputation.

At the same time, its educational mission was not forgotten. Thanks to the veritable renaissance of the Botanical Garden near the end of the 1970s, there was an increase in activities and alliances with various groups aimed at introducing the wonders of botany to the general public.

Extending over seven decades, the development of the Garden was slow and sometimes difficult, but Brother Marie-Victorin's dream finally came true. The Montréal Botanical Garden, a true miracle, at a latitude where the climate is harsh, has become one of the great gardens of North America, a remarkable homage to the plant kingdom the world over.

One Garden, Several Missions

Since its beginnings, the Montréal Botanical Garden has been more than just a public exhibition of a fine collection of flowers, trees, and plants.

Its Scientific Mission

The botanical resources of the Garden form a collection of great scientific import and constitute one of the most extensive collections in the world.

Essential to the advancement of knowledge, scientific research has been – and remains more than ever – a key element of the Garden's activities. It has also played an important role in establishing the prestigious international reputation enjoyed by the Montréal Botanical Garden today.

Research is conducted thanks to the joint efforts of the Garden's team of botanists and the Plant Biology Research Institute of the University of Montréal, which is affiliated with the Botanical Garden.

Its Educational Mission

The educational mission of the Botanical Garden was particularly close to the heart of Marie-Victorin. He insisted on introducing botany to children from an early age and, more importantly, on making them aware of the marvels and fragility of nature. It is with that in mind that the now hugely popular Youth Gardens (garden plots where schoolchildren learn about horticulture) were founded. Furthermore, numerous presentations and activities held at the Garden are specifically designed for young people.

The educational mission of the Garden is also aimed at adults. The Montréal Botanical Garden School of Horticulture, which is associated with the Botanical Garden, trains horticultural workers at all levels including those specializing in ornamental horticulture.

With over a million visitors annually, the Botanical Garden has become one of Montréal's main tourist attractions and is one of a group of four institutions dedicated to spreading a popular scientific and ecological culture. The Biodome has recreated four different ecosystems so that visitors can discover the

△   *Tree peony flower.*

◁   *The Flowery Brook, in early spring.*

diversity and importance of plant and animal life. The Insectarium, situated on the site of the Botanical Garden, presents the world of insects and arthropods using stimulating interactive displays. The Planetarium, located in the downtown area, provides visitors with the chance to discover the infinity of the cosmos. Together, these four institutions, managed by the Scientific Institutions Service of the City of Montréal, form the largest natural science museum complex in Canada.

Furthermore, the Garden is an ideal place for continuing education. Aware of the importance of putting names to what we observe in the world around us and understanding that world, it strives to enhance visitors' knowledge of the environment. Numerous associations, such as the Friends of the Botanical Garden and the Young Naturalists Club, collaborate on a regular basis in organizing thematic tours and educational activities in which thousands of groups of all ages participate every year.

Its Social and Cultural Mission

The activities of the Garden extend well beyond the bounds of botany and horticulture. Throughout the year, the various outdoor exhibitions and activities held at the Garden attract a wide range of visitors.

As the city's "environmental conscience," the Garden plays a fundamental role in creating a greener Montréal. Very much involved in city planning, it has developed a special relationship with the population and has contributed to the beautification of the city of Montréal.

Lastly, the Garden exposes visitors to cultures from all over the world. This is particularly evident in the remarkable success of its Japanese, Chinese, and First Nations Gardens. These gardens are not only magnificent and true recreations of landscapes unfamiliar to most people, they are also the backdrop for cultural activities that take place in the Garden. They are peaceful havens where, for example, visitors may expand their knowledge of Japanese painting, the Chinese language, or Amerindian and Inuit traditions.

▷ *Pansies 'Sorbet Purple Duet'.*

▽ *Yellow iris (Iris pseudacorus).*

2

A TOUR OF THE GARDEN

The Reception Gardens

Entering the Montréal Botanical Garden is like stepping into an oasis of greenery and flowers in the heart of the city. It is a discovery of lush vegetation of every fragrance and colour possible that takes you on a fascinating trip around the world.

With its 75 hectares of lawns, trees, and plants, and its ten exhibition greenhouses, the Montréal Botanical Garden ranks as one of the largest and finest gardens in the world.

The southwest entrance of the Botanical Garden opens onto the Reception Gardens. These gardens give visitors a foretaste of the highly diverse vegetation that is to come, both in the greenhouses and the vast outdoor spaces of the Garden – 21,000 species and varieties of plants from all over the world.

In front of the Administration Building, spreading out to the right and left, are magnificent geometric flower gardens dotted with fountains. Depending on the season, the gardens are filled with a wide variety of tulips and other bulb plants, or annuals of every colour and arran-

gement imaginable. There are also several exotic trees growing here at the northern limit of their hardiness zone – the kobus magnolia (*Magnolia kobus*), the tulip tree (*Liriodendron tulipifera*) and the dawn redwood (*Metasequoia glyptostroboides*).

To the right when you enter is a statue of Brother Marie-Victorin, eminent botanist and founder of the Garden. At the far end of the Reception Gardens, you can see the horizontal outline of the administration pavilion adjoining the Reception Centre. This art deco building, constructed between 1932 and 1938, is decorated with bas-reliefs representing scenes of Amerindian life that illustrate how plants were used at the time of colonization.

The Reception Centre

A tour of the Botanical Garden should really begin in the Reception Centre. The warm and stimulating atmosphere of this modern building makes it an excellent starting point for a journey into the fascinating world of plants.

A large-scale model gives you a view of the entire grounds, and visitors often use it to plan their own personal tour.

The Reception Centre contains a horticultural information counter, where visitors can consult specialized personnel for tips on choosing plants for their own garden and caring for them. An auditorium, a room to accommodate groups, and a library are also located in this building. In addition, it houses the "L'Orchidée" Gift Shop, where a large variety of souvenirs and a vast selection of books on horticulture and botany are available.

△ *Drawing of the Reception Centre by architect Lucien F. Kérouak, 1932.*

◁ *Summer cypresses, feathered cockscombs and flossflowers.*

The Greenhouses

The first block of exhibition greenhouses was built in 1956. Today visitors have the choice of ten greenhouses where they can explore a spectacular array of flowers from all over the world and discover exotic plants and trees that could not survive the rigours of our climate. They flourish within these glass walls, in a setting that resembles the equatorial or tropical habitats from which they originate.

More than 36,000 plants, representing 12,000 different species and varieties, grow in the greenhouses. This is a world of palm trees, banana trees, orchids, cacti, ferns, begonias, and penjings. Visitors can travel to the four corners of the earth, especially to the warmer regions of our planet. The Greenhouses are particularly enjoyable on a February morning when it's -20˚C outside! Let's not forget that they are open all year-round.

The Molson Hospitality Greenhouse

The Molson Hospitality Greenhouse is, so to speak, the gateway to the exhibition greenhouse complex and an invitation to discover the plant world. The main themes of reproduction, nutrition, and protection are presented using exhibit modules and interpretation panels that are placed along the paths.

The Molson Hospitality Greenhouse houses a collection of mono-cotyledons. This class is made up of plants such as palm trees, banana trees and bamboo – plants that, like corn, are characterized by parallel-veined leaves that form a sheath

△ Red ginger (Alpinia purpurata) inflorescence.

◁ Solitaire palm (Ptychosperma elegans) in the Molson Hospitality Greenhouse.

around the stem, and by their floral parts, which come in groups of three. Visitors are sure to be drawn to a terrarium of carnivorous plants that are utterly fascinating. At the back of the Molson Hospitality Greenhouse is the entrance to the Chlorophyll Room, which contains an exhibit specifically designed for children aged 6 to 11.

The greenhouses are situated on either side of the Molson Hospitality Greenhouse. The tour begins in the East Wing, at the entrance to the Tropical Rain Forest Conservatory.

The Tropical Rain Forest Conservatory

It's no easy task to reproduce a tropical rainforest, where the trees are usually immense, in a greenhouse that is barely five metres high. An ingenious method had to be used to recreate this type of vegetation. Trees were constructed using metal forms covered with sphagnum moss and cork, to which epiphytes were then attached. Epiphytes are plants that grow on trees without taking nourishment from them, using them only for physical support. Growing this way, they receive more rain and light than they would on the rainforest floor. The conservatory is set up so that visitors are at the level of the canopy of the trees and can therefore observe the plants living there.

In addition to a large collection of bromeliads, some orchids and ferns grow in this tropical setting. The visitors will also notice an intriguing greyish plant, known as Spanish moss (Tillandsia usneoides), which hangs from the trees. This epiphyte native to tropical forests is rootless and captures moisture in the ambient air with the aid of minuscule scales that are spread all over its surface.

△ Silver nerve plant (Fittonia verschaffeltii var. argyronewa), a common house plant.

△ Neoregelia 'Spring Song' (Neoregelia).

▽ Urn plant (Aechmea fasciata). This plant only flowers once, but before dying off it grows a sucker that will give rise to another plant.

The Economic Tropical Plants Conservatory

The next greenhouse is designed to familiarize visitors with commonly used trees and plants, such as the cacao tree, pepper plant, cinnamon tree, and coffee tree. These are referred to as "economic" plants, i.e. plants that humans grow for their own direct use.

In this conservatory visitors can discover, smell, and examine some 125 plants and trees that are used for food, condiments, medicine, etc. Not only is this equatorial vegetation beautiful and exotic, it also satisfies the practical needs of the daily lives of men and women the world over.

It is also in this greenhouse that visitors can really experience the all-enveloping atmosphere of a dense tropical forest and enjoy the olfactory, tactile, and visual sensations it affords. It is important that you take the time to read the interpretation panels and, above all, carefully observe your surroundings to get the most out of this conservatory. Look up and you might see a bunch of bananas; scan the borders and you might spot a pineapple. Perhaps the vanilla plant will be in bloom and you will be surprised to discover that it is really an orchid.

Natural Seduction

The extraordinary beauty of orchids and their astonishing shapes are no accident of nature. Orchids have a vast array of features designed to attract the insects that pollinate them. Their colour, shape and fragrance all make them easier to locate. It's a matter of survival!

The Orchids and Aroids Conservatory

A reproduction of the ruins of an ancient Latin American fortress that has been gradually overgrown with vegetation forms a fascinating backdrop for the exotic plants and flowers in this greenhouse. Original cobblestones dating back 300 years, taken from the streets of Old Montréal, have been recycled in stone walls of colonial inspiration.

Orchids belong to the largest family of flowering plants, and this is definitely the place to see and smell them! The plants seen here are only part of the Botanical Garden's prestigious collection, which includes some 1,500 different species and hybrids, for a total of 5,000 specimens. Orchids can flower for periods of several days to six months, depending on the species. Only specimens in bloom are displayed; after that, they are returned to the production greenhouse. The Sobralia, for example, only blooms for a day, whereas the Phalaenopsis flowers for two to three months (and sometimes longer)! So there are always orchids in flower in this greenhouse, but the greatest number of blooms can be seen between February and May, when they put on a breathtaking show of colours and shapes.

▽ *Three different orchids. From top to bottom:* Paphiopedilum hennisianum, Miltonia 'Cascade', Phalaenopsis 'Desert Dreams'. *The Garden's first collection of orchids was begun by Henry Teuscher in the 1940s. These plants, which have remained intact today, are remarkable in their age and size.*

The orchids are very different from the other major group of plants in this conservatory, the spectacular anthuriums. These plants, members of the aroid family, are characterized by a spike-shaped inflorescence (spadix), enclosed in an often brightly coloured sheathing leaf called a spathe.

The Ferns Conservatory

You are now entering the ancient and mysterious world of tropical ferns. These prehistoric plants appeared on earth before dinosaurs, but have outlived them by far.

Ferns are the oldest plants on our planet. For over 410 million years, these flowerless plants have spread to all parts of the globe, reproducing by means of spores. They come in a seemingly infinite variety of shades and shapes. Arborescent or herbaceous, aquatic or terrestrial, large or small, they fan out to provide a festival of lace.

Artificial rocks and a waterfall give this conservatory the sense of movement and sound that contributes to its ambience. Rocks, after all, have been the natural habitat of ferns since time began. Over the course of thousands of years, ferns have left behind numerous fossils, making it possible to trace them back to the Palaeozoic era.

The collection of ferns in the Botanical Garden includes 75 genera, 200 species, and 30 cultivars. In order to create a favourable environment for these plants, the temperature is kept at 22°C and the relative humidity at 70%.

The Begonias
and Gesneriads Conservatory

You now have to double back into the Molson Hospitality Greenhouse to reach the West Wing of the green-

△ Ferns, the oldest plants on our planet, reproduce by means of spores.

house complex, where you begin with the Begonias and Gesneriads Conservatory.

Everyone has heard of begonias, those annuals that often brighten balconies and flower beds. They are a favourite because of the diverse textures and shapes of their leaves. But how many people know that there are more than a thousand species of begonias? At the Botanical Garden, 220 species and 250 cultivars are grown – representing the Garden's widest collection.

The most common gesneriads are without a doubt African violets. But visitors will also be entranced in this conservatory by the columneas, gloxinias, and hanging plants with their flamboyant flowers. There are approximately one hundred species of gesneriads in this greenhouse, displaying a wide range of unusual shapes, textures, and colours.

The Arid Regions Conservatory
After having experienced the lush climate found in the hot, humid regions of the world, what a contrast this greenhouse is! You are suddenly in the arid world of Arizona, Mexico, and the large desert regions of Africa, home to cacti, agaves, euphorbias, and aloes.

From one continent to another, some of the varieties, such as the cacti (American) and the euphorbia

▷ *From top to bottom: three begonias* (Begonia *'Preussen'*, B. dominicalis, B. listada) *and a basket plant* (Aeschynanthus speciosus).

(African), are astonishingly similar, since they have evolved the same way. While these plants are all different, they all use the same strategies to adapt to the extreme climatic conditions in which they grow (blazing sun during the day and freezing cloudless nights).

Take a moment to observe one of the main differences between American cacti and African euphorbias, whose general appearance are really very similar: cacti have several needles grouped together, whereas euphorbias have spines grouped in pairs.

Faced with extremely arid conditions, these succulents are true survivors. Their fleshy stems store water

△ *Giant Mexican cereus (*Pachycereus pringle*i).*

and their leaves are reduced to spines or covered with a waxy film to limit evaporation. A striking example of plants adapted to their environment!

The Hacienda

The next greenhouse takes you to Mexico. In an all-white Hispanic decor, the Hacienda is very much a continuation of the previous greenhouse. It has been nicknamed the "Sunlight Conservatory"! Once again, cacti and succulents are the main attraction.

The smaller specimens are all together in a display case. Notice the lithops, these "living stones" that can survive in temperatures as high as 70°C. Their resemblance to stones and their ability to "hide" protect them from herbivores.

The Hacienda is also home to the remarkable pincushion cacti, plants that are particularly well adapted to the extreme temperatures of the higher altitudes of Mexico.

The Garden of Weedlessness

The plants in the next greenhouse, the Garden of Weedlessness, come from across the Pacific and give you a taste of what is to come in the Japanese and Chinese Gardens.

Here, visitors can become familiar with penjings. Penjings are the Chinese cousins of Japanese bonsai, the miniature trees that became popular in the West in the 1970s. The Montréal Botanical Garden's collection of these trees dates back to 1976 and represents one of the largest of its kind in the Western world.

*Nepal firethorn (*Pyracantha crenulata*): 35 years old.*

A special technique is used to grow these trees. If they were growing in their natural state, they would be the size of the trees in our yards. To keep them small enough for their pots, their branches and roots are very carefully pruned and the new growth is pinched off.

To the right as you enter the greenhouse are some miniature penjings displayed on a shelf. They are said to be miniature because they are even smaller than ordinary penjings – in fact, they can fit into the palm of your hand!

*Chinese podocarp (*Podocarpus macrophyllus*): 120 years old.*

The Garden of Weedlessness was specially built in 1985 to accommodate the superb collection of penjings donated by Wu Yee-Sun of Hong Kong, an eminent bonsai expert and intellectual master of the Lingnan School of Southern China. During the summer, you can also see bonsai and penjings in the Chinese Garden, the Japanese Garden, and the Tree House.

*Chinese podocarp (*Podocarpus macrophyllus*): 40 years old.*

Main Exhibition Greenhouse
You have finally arrived at the last (but not the least important) greenhouse: the Main Exhibition

*Chinese landscape (*axinite stone*).*

33

△ Java glorybower (Clerodendrum speciosissimum).

◁ Tailed jay (Graphium agamemnon) during the "Butterflies Go Free" event.

▽ Thematic exhibition in the Main Exhibition Greenhouse: a Noah's Ark to preserve plant diversity.

Greenhouse, which is reserved for seasonal events. It is 13 metres high and its two levels cover an area of 700 square meters. Three or four times a year, the floral decor is changed according to the season.

In March it's time to celebrate the arrival of spring: hyacinths, hydrangeas, tulips, and azaleas fill the greenhouse with blazing colour. In June, the touch-me-nots, coleus, and other summer plants arrive. The fall celebrates mystery and fairy tales, when children are invited to the "Great Pumpkin Ball", which takes place among thousands of blooming chrysanthemums. A special win-

ter event is held at Christmas, followed by "Butterflies Go Free" when, in collaboration with the Insectarium, beautiful tropical butterflies are released into the greenhouse. Visitors can stroll around this tropical paradise, enjoying the sight of butterflies flying free.

Behind the Scenes

In addition to the greenhouses mentioned so far, the Botanical Garden has a 10,000-square-metre greenhouse complex (that is not open to the public), where its collections are kept and plants are grown for the

▷ *Following pages: climbing roses 'Sympathie' and 'Félicité et Perpétue'.*

various exhibitions throughout the year. These greenhouses contain nearly 20,000 plants that are taken care of by about 20 horticulturists.

The Rose Garden

Let's step outside now, to the vast outdoor gardens that spread over a 75-hectare area. Although some say that winter lasts six months in Québec, visitors still have well over half a year to admire the beauty and diversity of these gardens!

The rose, the queen of all flowers, is given the royal treatment at the Botanical Garden. Established in 1976, the Rose Garden covers 6 hectares and contains no less than 10,000 rose bushes, providing a show of blooms from the end of May to the first frost in October.

Guarding the entrance to the Rose Garden is a huge two-ton sculpture of a lion atop a pedestal surrounded by roses. This regal bronze lion was a gift from the city of Lyon in France to mark the 350th anniversary, in 1992, of the founding of Montréal.

Completely modern in design, the Rose Garden is laid out in winding beds rather than the more traditional straight rows. It forms a kaleidoscope of colours that invites visitors

The Rose Collection

Throughout the long history of roses, impassioned collectors have devoted their lives to crossing different varieties to create new cultivars. The Botanical Garden's collection of roses includes 220 cultivars of modern strains (hybrid tea roses, floribunda, grandiflora, miniature, and climbing roses), 450 cultivars of modern shrub roses, 180 cultivars of old garden roses, and 160 botanical species.

Photo: Réjean Martel, JBM

△   *At the top in the center: hybrid tea rose 'Sunset Celebration'.*
    From left to right: hybrid tea roses 'Blue Girl', 'Timeless', 'Maria Stern', and 'Montréal'.

to discover the diversity of the world of roses. Synonymous with beauty, roses come in an astounding variety of sizes, colours, and fragrances – some subtle, some strong.

One notable feature of the Rose Garden is the fact that it is situated at such a northerly latitude. It is no easy task to grow the fragile cultivars of modern strains in Canadian zone 5b, where winters are sometimes very cold. Since these magnificent plants are sensitive to frost, they are covered in the autumn with huge thermal blankets.

In 1992 a new section was added especially for botanical roses – simpler, highly scented species that grow in a natural environment. After various crossings, these rosebushes produced countless varieties and cultivars.

Modern shrub roses are well represented at the Botanical Garden, including specimens from Agriculture Canada's "Explorers" and "Parkland" series, roses developed by Dr. Griffith Buck, and English roses. In the section that displays R. rugosa hybrid roses, there are over 60 varieties and cultivars. The collection of old garden roses includes the largest groups (hardy in zone 5b) in the history of the breeding of this fragrant flower.

Another feature that makes this garden different from a traditional rose garden: the roses have been planted in a setting of shrubs and trees, which may sometimes be overlooked because of the striking beauty of the flowers themselves. But visitors should take a moment to appreciate the fragrance of the mock orange (Philadelphus spp.) when it is in bloom in June, to admire the exceptional honey locust (Gleditsia triacanthos), or to see the scarlet oak (Quercus coccinea) turn crimson in the autumn. These shrubs and trees give the Rose Garden its natural look, ensuring it blends in perfectly with the rest of the Botanical Garden.

△ *A more traditional part of the Rose Garden, set aside especially for old roses.*

▷ *Following page: honey locust (Gleditsia triancanthos).*

The Forest of the Montréals of France

The Botanical Garden created the Forest of the Montréals of France in 1992 to mark the 350th anniversary of the founding of Montréal. For the occasion, six towns in France named "Montréal" donated trees typical to their region. As a result, this section of the Botanical Garden contains 23 species of trees that represent each of these regions.

The garden gives visitors a visual image of the location of the regions represented. On a flagstone map of France, showing the locations of all the Montréals, the mayors have left their handprints for posterity at the exact location of their town. The Forest of the Montréals of France is a symbol of the friendship and historical bond between Québec and France, the land of its forefathers.

This area is also home to a small collection of modern garden roses, including some hybrid tea roses from France, and shrub roses belonging to the "Meidiland" series.

The Marsh and Bog Garden

This garden features aquatic and wetland plants that grow in Quebec, and others from more exotic parts. The above-ground basins provide a good view of plants that visitors would normally have difficulty observing in their natural environment without getting their feet wet. Among other things, visitors can enjoy the spectacle of white, mauve, and pink water lilies creating a floating carpet of harmonious colour. When the sacred lotus (*Nelumbo nucifera*) and water hyacinth (*Eichhornia crassipes*) are in bloom, in August, it is a sight not to be missed!

The Chinese Garden

One of the jewels of the Montréal Botanical Garden is, without a doubt, the spectacular Chinese Garden, opened in June 1991. This garden is the largest of its kind outside of China. It was designed by the renowned Chinese architect, Le Weizhong, who drew his inspiration directly from private gardens that were popular during the Ming dynasty (14th to 17th centuries) and that can still be seen in the southern region of Yangzi.

Composed of plants, stone, water, and traditional architecture, this garden has neither the lawns of an English garden nor the precise lines of a French garden, but illustrates the contrast between *yin* and *yang*. Unlike Western gardens, which lean toward conventional symmetry, a traditional Chinese garden favours an asymmetrical design. Clearly delineated, the Chinese Garden covers 2.5 hectares and has no less than seven pavilions. Some of them have highly poetic names and all are of great architectural interest.

This garden is the fruit of bonds forged between Montréal and Shanghai, the twinned cities that worked jointly on the project. It was, for the most part, built in China and shipped to Montréal in pieces. Some 120 containers carrying 2,500 tons of material – including 500 tons of grey stone shaped by the waters of

△ *Branch of flowering almond (Prunus triloba 'Multiplex').*

▷ *The Moon-shaped Door.*

Tai Lake – arrived in the port of Montréal from China by boat. The pieces were assembled throughout 1990 by some 50 craftsmen from Shanghai, who came to assist employees of the Montréal Botanical Garden. The garden was finally opened at the beginning of the following summer.

The Entrance Courtyard

You enter this peaceful garden through the Entrance Courtyard. From the Rose Garden, you take a small curved pathway that leads to a four-ton boulder, inscribed with the name of the garden in Chinese: *Meng hu*, which means "Dream Lake Garden." A homonym of *Meng hu* is "Montréal-Shanghai Garden."

Two symbols of authority, a male and a female lion carved out of stone, guard the entrance to the garden. As you enter, you notice on the ground the mosaic made of polished pebbles, crushed stone, and hand-made fragments of clay – a true masterpiece of traditional craftsmanship.

Facing the entrance are three tall stones that come from the bottom of Tai Lake. They represent the Three Stars, ancient Chinese deities that symbolize the search for happiness (the stone on the right), prosperity (the stone in the centre), and longevity (the stone on the left).

To the right of the entrance is a grand kobus magnolia more than 40 years old. The magnolia, which has traditionally symbolized wealth, is the emblem of the city of Shanghai. On the other side is a large Oriental thuja. The Entrance Courtyard also contains a flowering crabapple (symbol of Montréal), a Russian olive tree, a banana tree, and a stand of bamboo – a plant that bends but does not break, another symbol of Confucian wisdom.

The mural of grey brick on the left depicts crested cranes that have flown across the seas from Shanghai to alight on the maples of Montréal. The four Chinese characters on the mural read *He wu feng yin*, which means "the cranes dance in the shade of the maples."

The Moon-shaped Door

At the back of the courtyard, farther to the left, is the Moon-shaped Door that takes you out of the Entrance Courtyard, from where you get a lovely overall view of the entire Chinese Garden. To the left, there is a small zigzagging bridge, said to drive away evil spirits (who travel only in straight lines!), that leads to the Friendship Hall, the main structure in the garden. Among the plants and trees in this section, just before you cross the bridge, are a Manchurian walnut and a Chinese catalpa.

△   *The Friendship Hall with the tower of the Olympic Stadium in the background, illustrating the friendship that has been forged between Shanghai et Montréal.*

◁   *Snowdrop windflowers (Anemone sylvestris).*

The Friendship Hall

The characters on the plaque above the doors of the Friendship Hall read *Qin yi tang*, which literally means "Room of Close Friendship."

Forming the centrepiece of the Chinese Garden, the Friendship Hall is a fine example of the type of architecture that was prevalent during the Ming dynasty. This formidable building of some 100 square metres is made up of a wooden structure with numerous windows and a roof of baked clay tiles treated with iron oxide to harden them. It is a showpiece of thousand-year-old Chinese architecture, beautifully balanced with its distribution of weight over the entire structure.

The orientation of the Hall is very important: the entrance must face south – according to an ancient Chinese law, a building that turns its back to the sun risks attracting unfavourable influences.

You come into the Hall the same way you leave – thus abiding by a Chinese superstition that recommends stepping over the threshold without placing your foot on it, lest you attract bad luck!

Inside, the very simple furnishings consist of wooden tables, couches, and stools. The Friendship Hall regularly hosts exhibitions held at the Garden. Depending on the occasion, these temporary exhibitions showcase various artefacts of Chinese culture, such as paintings, photographs, handcrafted objects, lanterns, ancient coins, etc.

If you turn to look back as you step onto the terrace, you will see a

The Peony and the Lotus

In China, the tree peony (*Paeonia suffruticosa*) represents aristocracy and wealth. Grown for centuries, this flower even attracted the attention of Marco Polo back in the 13th century! The sacred lotus (*Nelumbo nucifera*) symbolizes the soul fighting against the material world and the tyranny of emotions. It is also called the "flower of Buddha" since Buddha is often represented sitting on a throne of lotus flowers.

Photo: Gilbert Morel, JBM

47

finely carved frieze over the gallery. From the terrace, you get the most spectacular view of the Chinese Garden: the mountain, rising above Dream Lake. To construct this nine-metre high mountain, 3,000 tons of yellowish stone was taken from Île Sainte-Hélène. A waterfall makes a superb contrast to the stone, creating a soothing environment.

The Springtime Courtyard

The next stop is the Springtime Courtyard, which can be reached from the Friendship Hall by following a little path bordered by irises and a Kuriles cherry tree.

The Springtime Courtyard contains part of the Garden's collection of penjings. Here you will see them in miniaturized landscapes, where arrangements of stones represent mountains, and basins of water represent lakes and rivers. The Springtime Courtyard looks directly out onto the Lotus Pavilion. Lotus, aquatic plants that are typically Chinese, have great symbolic and religious connotation. This pavilion houses the Chinese Garden's gift shop.

"The Magic of Lanterns"

Much more than an array of sights and fragrances, the Chinese Garden is also the scene of various cultural events and activities. For example, Chinese language courses are given here. Every autumn, as the evenings get darker, a dazzling exhibition of lanterns is held in this entrancing site.

△ *The Green Shade Pavilion.*

The Green Shade Pavilion

The Green Shade Pavilion is situated behind the Lotus Pavilion, set back and perched atop a small hill. From here you can take in a view of the Chinese Garden. As you walk along the path that leads to the pavilion, take a moment to look at the white mulberry. In the summer it produces fat, black berries that birds love. In China, the leaves of the mulberry provide nourishment for silkworms.

After your stop at the Green Shade Pavilion, go along Dream Lake until you get to the Stone Mountain. There are pathways that lead up the mountain.

The Tower of Condensing Clouds

Behind the Stone Mountain is the Tower of Condensing Clouds. It resembles a pagoda – a building that is associated with Chinese architecture but in fact originates in India (pagodas were inspired by the Indian stupa, a bell-shaped monument). Flanking the Tower of Condensing Clouds are crabapple

△ *The Pavilion of Infinite Pleasantness.*

△ *The Stone Boat.*

trees, smoketrees, and an Austrian pine.

As you continue your walk around the lake, you will notice crabapple trees and a purple-leafed sand cherry tree. To the left of the path is the Pavilion of Infinite Pleasantness, where you can see a Jack pine and a weeping willow leaning over the lake.

The Stone Boat

The last pavilion in the Chinese Garden is the Stone Boat, which seems to be almost floating on Lotus Pond like a boat lying at anchor. With its sail, the little terrace in the "bow" looks like the deck of a boat. From here you can enjoy a spectacular view of the entire Chinese Garden, a fitting way to conclude your tour.

The Japanese Garden

The Japanese Garden officially opened on June 28, 1988, but there had been talk of a Japanese garden in Montréal long before that time. Twenty-one years before, Ken Nakajima, a renowned Japanese architect and one of the masters of Japan's Modern School of Landscape Architecture, had been asked to design a Japanese garden for the Botanical Garden for the 1967 World Exhibition (Expo 67). The plans were a gift from the Japanese Committee of Montréal for the 100th anniversary of Canadian Confederation, but for various reasons, the project was not carried out. The idea was not forgotten, however, and 20 years later the project resurfaced. The plans were amended and adapted and work was begun.

Everything must be in harmony in a Japanese garden. Nothing is left to chance. Although more contemporary than the Chinese Garden, the Japanese Garden also represents traditional, even eternal, values. This oasis of tranquillity uses water, rock, and plants to express the Japanese concept of inner peace.

▷ *Japanese lantern with a small shaped Amur maple.*

▽ *The Japanese Pavilion.*

Stone

Stone, one of the fundamental elements of the art of Japanese landscaping, is a symbol of longevity and the presence of forces of nature. Stone anchors the garden to the ground and shapes its personality. The stones are set out according to their size and shape and in accordance with strict rules full of symbolism. They are sometimes laid out in pairs, but more frequently in groups of 3, 5 or 7.

The choice of the type of stone to be used was a decisive stage in the design of the garden. After much searching, Ken Nakajima found a stone suitable for his design in a deposit at Thetford Mines, in the heart of the asbestos region of Québec.

Some 500 tons of peridotite were extracted to build the Japanese Garden. Peridotite, a smooth greenish rock with black and white streaks, produces a spectacular effect. It goes well not only with plants and trees, but also with streams and ponds, and was used to build the waterfall that forms the centrepiece of the garden.

Water

Water, another important element in Japanese landscape art, is used to express the beauty of nature. It is a symbol of renewal, peace, and the wonder and continuity of the hereafter. In the Japanese Garden, water fills the ponds, flows over falls, and runs in the brooks. Little bridges

cross the water in various places, creating pleasant spots to pause and admire the scenery, feel the soft breeze, and observe the carp swimming in the water below.

Koi carps have been admired for centuries by the Japanese, who call them "living flowers." Today they crossbreed them, producing highly valued specimens. Contests are held and they are judged according to their colour, the number and pattern of their spots, and the beauty of their scales.

On the side of the pond is a Kotoji, or tuning fork lantern, which has one foot on the ground and the other in water. It was originally used to guide visitors during nocturnal celebrations. The light it gave

off was seen as the light of knowledge that dispels the clouds of ignorance.

▽ *Plants (azaleas), stone (axinite) and water in harmony near the waterfall.*

△ *The Small Soan Pavilion.*

▽ *Koi carp.*

Plants

A proper Japanese garden is attractive in all seasons, displaying a constant succession of blooms: crabapples, rhododendrons, peonies, irises, white water lilies, and lotus all have their moment in the sun. Evergreens provide greenery all year-round.

The plants in the Japanese Garden are cared for in the same way as bonsai: as they grow, they are shaped to correspond exactly to the graphic or symbol desired.

One of the greatest horticultural challenges in building this garden was finding plants that were aesthetically equivalent to Japanese plants, but at the same time better adapted to our climate. Since the aim in creating the Japanese Garden

was to make it an idealized vision of nature, the designers tried to include native plants. In some cases, rather than plant Japanese maples (*Acer palmatum*), which are difficult to grow in our climate, they chose Amur maples (*Acer tataricum* ssp. *ginnala*). Cherry trees, grown widely in Japan and of which there were few, were replaced by crabapples and serviceberries, whose spring flowers are equally attractive.

The Japanese Pavilion

The Pavilion was opened on June 22, 1989, one year after the construction of the Japanese Garden. Its contemporary look is the work of Hisato Hirakoa, an architect from Osaka.

The Pavilion opens its doors to the cultural and artistic world of Japan. It hosts exhibitions and cultural events, and houses a tearoom where visitors can partake in traditional Japanese rites of hospitality.

A bonsai garden has been built in a courtyard adjacent to the Japanese Pavilion, where a large collection of miniature trees are grown according to the rules of this thousand-year-old art. Some of the specimens are truly ancient, ranging from 25 to 350 years old! A large part of the collection was generously donated to the Garden in 1989 by the Nippon Bonsai Association. From early spring to the end of the fall, visitors can admire the Japanese maple (*Acer palmatum*), as well as several junipers and azaleas in this collection.

The Pavilion looks out onto the Zen Garden. This garden combines sand and stone – peridotite from Thetford Mines and white sand imported from Kyoto. Eleven peridotite stones stand like islands in a sea of white sand. The Zen Garden is an ideal place for meditation. It also leads to a tea garden, an extension of the tearoom.

The Traditional Picnic

One of the activities organized annually in the Japanese Garden is the traditional picnic in May. You can reserve a Japanese-style boxed lunch and enjoy it under the flowering crabapples in the garden, and thus experience a tradition that has been practiced for centuries by Japanese families and lovers.

▽ *In June, irises, which thrive in a moist environment, brighten the edges of the brook.*

The Shade Garden

Very popular during the hot days of summer, the Shade Garden is nonetheless interesting from a botanical point of view. In this garden, visitors discover plants that can grow with a limited amount of light... and there are a lot of them! Its size and the variety of its collections make it one of the largest shade gardens in North America.

This garden used to grow under the shade of majestic elm trees. But in the 1970s and 1980s, a horticultural catastrophe occurred when Dutch elm disease decimated the species all over North America. It destroyed the trees that provided cover for the Shade Garden, and they were subsequently replaced with maples, ash trees, and linden trees.

It is in this garden that the first flowers of spring appear, blooming before leaves grow on the trees when there is more light. Primroses, native plants (Jack-in-the-pulpit, liverleaf, bloodroot, etc.), and bulbs form an impressive carpet of colour, all competing to provide a beautiful show.

The spring flowers make way for astilbes, cranesbills, plantain lilies, and ferns in the summer. The ferns are a particularly spectacular sight in shade gardens. In the autumn, their fruit, flowers, and leaves provide a festival of colour, combining yellows, oranges, ochres, and purples.

△ *Left: Japanese primrose (*Primula japonica*). Right: Large-flower dead-nettle (*Lamium orvala*).*

The Insectarium

Like the Botanical Garden, the Insectarium is part of the Scientific Institutions Service of the City of Montréal.

Opened in 1990, it is one of Montréal's treasures of popular scientific culture. It houses an extraordinary collection of some 160,000 insects and arthropods, both live and mounted. Most of this important collection was donated by Georges Brossard, founder of the Insectarium.

Every year, insect tastings are held, allowing visitors to experience the culinary traditions of peoples from all over the world. The event always attracts a lot of interest, even if the enthusiasm for taking part is not always unanimous!

The gardens surrounding the Insectarium have been specifically designed to include plants that attract butterflies and bees. During the summer months, visitors can stroll through the Butterfly House where hundreds of butterflies native to Québec flutter among the nectar-bearing flowers.

The Tree House

A stop at this pavilion, set in the northeast corner of the Botanical Garden, will help visitors understand the importance of trees and wood, in our lives and in the history of humanity. Opened in 1996, the Tree House is almost entirely built out of wood in an original, contemporary architectural design.

This small interpretation centre presents trees from a biological, economic, and cultural perspective. The permanent exhibition, "At the Heart of the Tree," shows all aspects of a tree, from its growth rings to its countless uses in our daily life. Temporary exhibitions on specific themes are held regularly.

The Tree House is also home to a collection of North American bonsai.

The Arboretum

A rboretum is a Latin word meaning "an area planted with trees." The Botanical Garden's arboretum covers nearly half of all the grounds, a tribute to the plant that Beethoven often said he preferred to man.

All types of trees and shrubs that can grow at our latitude are found here – some 7,000 specimens belonging to 2,000 different species. They are grouped by family and genus and are all labelled to assist visitors in identifying the various species, with

red plaques indicating the more exceptional specimens.

The Arboretum changes with the seasons. In the springtime, the crabapples in bloom create a striking effect. In the summer, the willows along the sides of the ponds grab our attention. In the fall, various trees and shrubs – mountain ash, spindle trees, etc. – are covered with colourful fruit. In the winter, in addition to providing popular cross-country ski trails, the Arboretum becomes an ideal place for bird-watching.

The largest tree in the Montréal Botanical Garden is an Eastern cot-

△ *Fruits of a spindle tree.*

tonwood (Populus deltoides), a tree that was growing on the grounds well before the Garden came into being. It is approximately 28 metres high, and its trunk is 1.38 metres in diameter. The cottonwood is located just in front of the Rose Garden.

The Leslie Hancock Garden

Nestled in the heart of the Arboretum is the Leslie Hancock Garden, home to members of the *Ericaceae* (heath) family (rhododendrons, heathers, azaleas, etc.). Leslie Hancock (1892-1977) was a prominent breeder of rhododendrons. He introduced new cultivars and played an active role in creating the collection of *Ericaceae* at the Botanical Garden.

The conifers surrounding this garden form a screen of vegetation that catches the snow and protects these somewhat fragile plants from cold winds. Because of the conifers, the rhododendrons in the Leslie Hancock Garden form one of the northern-most collections of rhododendrons in the world. This spot offers an exceptional show of colour twice a year – in mid-May when the foamflowers form carpets of white blossoms beneath the Japanese azaleas in full bloom, and then at the beginning of June when the rhododendrons are in their splendour.

While the rhododendrons and azaleas are the main attraction of this garden, they are not the only members of the heath family found here. There are also other heaths, heathers, and wintergreen (*Gaultheria procumbens*) – all species that belong to the same large family, of which the blueberry is a particularly tasty example. No annuals are grown in this garden, with the exception of some pansies that add colour to the flower beds.

The Flowery Brook

The Flowery Brook, situated between the Alpine Garden and the Ponds, is just as its name suggests. A brook winds its way through flower beds that display a profusion of blooms. Visitors walk on the grass, stepping over little bridges that give the garden a pastoral look.

This garden was planted according to the style of a traditional English garden. Contrary to the formal style of a French garden (of which the gardens at Versailles, created by Le Nôtre, are one of the most spectacular examples), English gardens follow no rules of symmetry, and their lines are curved, not straight.

The Flowery Brook is laid out along paths lined with trees native to the eastern part of North America, such as the American hornbeam (*Carpinus caroliniana*), the ironwood (*Ostrya virginiana*), and, near the ponds, the hackberry (*Celtis occidentalis*). Here visitors can discover the ornamental value of trees indigenous to this area.

In addition to the irises, daylilies and peonies provide an impressive display. There are 613 species and cultivars of irises, 200 species of peonies and 244 species of daylilies. The best time to admire the irises and peonies is between June 1 and 15. The daylilies are in their glory between July 15 and 30. At these periods, the blooms are at their best and the colours and fragrances are particularly pronounced, but it is worth a trip to the Flowery Brook even outside those dates. In the spring, the bulbs flower, followed by a wide variety of perennials.

△   *From left to right: Japanese iris (Iris ensata), cardinal flower (Lobelia cardinalis).*

▽   *From left to right: asiatic lily 'Sun Ray' (Lilium 'Sun Ray'), daylily 'Tejas' (Hemerocallis 'Tejas').*

The Ponds

Two large ponds, located at the centre of the Montréal Botanical Garden, illustrate the harmony that is possible between vegetation and wildlife. The water, shrubs, and tall plants are natural attractions for birds. Numerous species – particularly ducks, bitterns, plovers, and blue herons – have chosen to make this their home, in the shade of the elegant weeping willows that grow along the east side of the ponds.

This is an ideal place for visitors to relax and enjoy the water, trees, and birds, not to mention the various species of aquatic plants, such as water lilies and blue flags, that thrive in this picturesque environment.

The Lilac Collection

The lilac collection of the Botanical Garden covers an area of 8,000 square metres. It is comprised of 3,000 bushes representing more than 180 cultivars and 19 different species. More than enough to make this a scent sensation you won't want to miss!

The First Nations Garden

Opened in 2001, the First Nations Garden illustrates the close bonds between the Amerindian and Inuit peoples and the plant world. A natural environment, this garden shows the milieu that was home to the eleven First Nations of Québec.

The concept for this garden has been evolving for more than a half a century. The layout of a garden containing "Indian" medicinal plants appeared in the initial plans drawn up by Brother Marie-Victorin and landscape architect Henry Teuscher. Marie-Victorin's successor, Jacques Rousseau, was a pioneer in the study of the Amerindians of Québec. But it took until 2001 before the garden was completed, in time for the 300th anniversary of the Great Peace Treaty of Montreal, which was signed at Pointe-à-Callière on August 4, 1701.

Throughout the entire design and building phases of the garden, the Botanical Garden worked in close

collaboration with a committee of First Nations representatives created specifically for the project.

The First Nations Garden is organized around several themes, all relating to the knowledge, cultivation, and uses of various plant species. It focuses not only on the know-how of the Amerindian and Inuit peoples, but also the plant-related activities they carried out: the gathering of plants for both consumption and medicinal purposes; the use of wood and trees to make objects; the transport and construction of dwellings; and the cultivation of food plants.

This garden can be divided into five sections: four designed for interpretation purposes and one for special activities. The first three sections recreate the main ecosystems found across the territories occupied by the First Nations: deciduous forests (in the Saint Lawrence Valley and south of the river), Laurentian and boreal forests, and the northern taiga and tundra. A pavilion located in the fourth section is used for presentations on the botanical and horticultural traditions of the First Nations and their wood processing methods – as they were practiced three centuries ago, and how they have evolved since that time with the introduction of contemporary technologies. This pavilion also contains a gift shop. The fifth section has been set up to accommodate gatherings and special events.

The Alpine Garden

A visit to the Alpine Garden is like hiking through the Caucasus, Pyrenees, Rockies, and Alps all at once! Even though the hillocks that make up this garden are relatively low, the surroundings make you feel like you are really on a mountain trail. Horticulturists have shaped the trees to make them look like they have had to adapt to the harsh climatic conditions of high altitudes.

Although work on this garden was first begun in 1936, it was only completed in the 1960s. The garden is centred around a huge rocky slope that features a cascading brook. Visitors can wander along the paths that wind around this mountain of stone and discover the eleven geographical sections that make up the garden. Each section corresponds to a mountainous region of the world and contains vegetation typical of that region. One feature common to all the plants and trees in this garden is that they grow at altitudes of over 1,000 metres. There is a distinction made between sub-alpine species that grow between altitudes of 1,500 and 2,000 metres, and alpine species that are found at altitudes of over 2,000 metres.

The central slopes are surrounded by sections that contain specific types of vegetation, such as dwarf evergreens or ground-covers. A mineralogical garden contains a collection of rocks and minerals that were displayed in the Canadian Pavilion during Expo 67.

▽ Left: edging candytuft (Iberis sempervirens) under an Austrian pine. Right: basket-of-gold (Aurinia saxatilis).

The Exhibition Gardens

Located along Boulevard Pie-IX on the west side of the Botanical Garden, the Exhibition Gardens are a succession of more traditional gardens. Their symmetrical layout reflects the orderly style of French gardens. Rather than being an expression of modern, bold, or exotic landscape design, they are intended for educational purposes. Even today, this section displays the mark of Henry Teuscher, who came up with the plans for the Botanical Garden with Brother Marie-Victorin and was the first curator of this important Montréal institution.

△ *From left to right: garden phlox, climbing honeysuckle 'Mandarin', patens clematis 'Wada's Primrose' and cannas.*

◁ *Previous pages: Globe thistle (Echinops sphaerocephalus).*

The Shrub Garden

This garden displays a collection of shrubs and hedges. The plants are carefully grouped by family and genus and provide a lovely display of flowering shrubs from spring to fall. The south side of the garden is graced by a collection of clematis.

The Poisonous Plant Garden

Dangerous plants that can cause poisoning, allergic reactions, and skin irritations are featured in this garden. This is where visitors learn to beware of ragweed, poison ivy, rhubarb (whose stem is edible, but whose leaf is toxic), and even lily of the valley!

The Medicinal Plant Garden

Sweet flag, common yarrow (*Achillea millefolium*), and purple trillium are just a few of the plants that have been used by people for centuries for their therapeutic properties. Today the use of plants is becoming more and more popular as a natural way of relieving pain and curing ailments, particularly those associated with the stresses of modern life.

This garden contains about 100 plants used in folk medicine or in the pharmaceutical industry which, we tend to forget, does not only use chemical compounds; it is also always in need of natural substances! Yellow gentian (Gentiana lutea) and common foxglove are two examples of medicinal plants that are produced commercially.

The Corner of Québec

Tucked away behind the Monastery Garden is a small garden that contains specimens of plants that are native to the Montréal area. The Botanical Garden is proud to display plants from all over the world, but has not forgotten those we are used to seeing in their natural state, plants whose names we often don't know.

Found here are indigenous species such as the common water plantain that grows in marshes, and the Jack-in-the-pulpit (*Arisaema triphyllum*), white trillium, and ferns that are typical of the undergrowth in the woodlands in and around Montréal. Fruit-bearing plants that attract birds in the summer are also found in this garden.

The Monastery Garden

Did you know that chervil, European wild ginger, and spearmint were the subject of laws during the Middle Ages? In an edict issued in 812, Charlemagne ordered that these plants be grown in the royal gardens. It was to remind visitors of the importance of medicinal and aromatic plants more than a thousand years ago that the Montréal Botanical Garden created this space devoted to species that were grown in monastery gardens during the Middle Ages.

The plants are arranged to resemble what we know of the monastery gardens. It would appear that ancient wisdom is alive and well because many of these plants are still widely popular.

The City Gardens

Visitors who are looking for new ideas for their own yard will enjoy this section of the Botanical Garden. Various landscaping designs are laid out here, each taking up an area about the size of an average city yard. Developed in collaboration with landscaping professionals, these gardens offer a host of ideas for transforming a backyard into a pleasant environment where flowers and greenery flourish in harmony. Each garden was designed according to a specific theme, and there is something to suit all tastes! Every year some of the gardens are

changed to present new ideas. The City Gardens are enough to convince any gardening enthusiast that you don't need to have a large estate to create a little oasis of greenery.

The Garden of Innovations

Its environment changing from year to year, this garden displays new trends in horticulture, whether they relate to plants, building materials, or landscape design. Here visitors can see the most interesting of the trees, shrubs, perennials, and annuals that are introduced on the market each year. This garden is the result of collaboration between the City of Montréal, Permacon, and the landscape architecture school at the University of Montréal, and benefits

from the participation of various landscaping suppliers.

The Lover's Bench

Under the shade of the linden trees in the Perennial Garden is a famous work of art, "The Lover's Bench," a sculpture by Canadian artist Lea Vivot that created a scandal in Toronto when it was first exhibited.

△ Recent sunflower varieties in the Garden of Innovations. From left to right: 'The Joker', 'Velvet Queen', 'Autumn Beauty'.

◁ The City Gardens.

79

The Economic Plant Garden

This garden illustrates the important role that plants have played in the economy in the past and in the present.

Textile plants, edible plants, forage crop plants, and tobacco plants are just a few of the sections that are laid out systematically in this garden, which forms an outdoor extension of the Economic Tropical Plants Conservatory. Corn, peanuts, vegetables, and plants used for dyes or textiles are all listed, classified, and described on panels that explain the history and use of each of the plants featured.

Visitors will also want to take a quick look at the Economic Plant Garden's sister garden on the other side of the road, the Knot Garden, where they can admire – but not taste – various herbs used as condiments, edible flowers, and some miniature vegetables. This is the perfect place to dis-cover the ornamental attributes of the vegetables grown at the Botanical Garden and to learn more about companion planting.

The Perennial Garden

Another source of ideas for home gardeners, the Perennial Garden is a carefully laid out selection of plants that are able to survive the seasons of our northerly latitude, all beautifully displayed among the linden trees, fountains, and pools.

The Perennial Garden is the oldest Exhibition Garden. Its long beds are filled with asters, phlox, and larkspurs, to name just a few of the plants that manage to survive our harsh winter. Only a few species – cannas, gladiola, and dahlias – are not frost-resistant and must be dug up and stored in greenhouses over the winter.

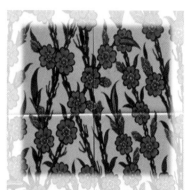

The Peace Garden

The Montréal Botanical Garden has always, but especially since the 1980s, been sensitive to other cultures in the world, and has often injected its projects with an international flavour. This time, it is Turkey and its native tulips that have provided the inspiration for this garden, which was inaugurated in the year 2000.

The Peace Garden is adorned with beautiful tiles bearing a floral design that come from Iznik, an ancient coastal city on the Marmara sea. Created using an authentic traditional technique, they decorate seven low walls and seven pillars. These tiles were a gift from the Turkish community in Montréal and the Iznik Foundation. Iznik tiles have been around for no less than nine centuries. The art of making these tiles was lost during the Renaissance but was re-created with amazing accuracy in the 1990s.

Every year, the arrival of spring is celebrated in the Peace Garden with a beautiful display of tulips.

The Courtyard of the Senses

Here, instead of the usual "please don't touch," the watchword is "Please touch and smell, but don't look!" Since it was opened in August 1999, the Courtyard of the Senses has sparked much interest. It was specifically designed for visually impaired visitors but all are welcome, of course – as long as you close your eyes.

The Courtyard of the Senses has four main "hands-on" exhibits that visitors are invited to discover using their sense of touch. Several plants that are characteristically prickly, soft, sticky, or rough are used to convey the different sensations. For example, the borage plant is used to illustrate "prickly" and the eucalyptus is used to convey "sticky".

▽   *Flat-leaved eryngo* (Eryngium planum).

APPENDICES

What the Future Holds for the Montréal Botanical Garden

A garden is constantly evolving. It follows the rhythm of the seasons and changes as new flowers come into bloom. Over the years it acquires maturity. Managing its collections effectively, making new acquisitions, selecting new and untried plants – to do all these things requires those who care for and improve the collections of plants to be aware of the latest advances in horticulture.

In Montréal, the Botanical Garden is busy working on new projects: for example, it is giving the Tree House and Arboretum sector a new look. There are plans to build a path in the Arboretum so that visitors can get a closer look at the trees and shrubs, and to install interpretation panels for subjects such as "trees in an urban setting," "birds", and "large collections of trees." Another interpretation path will be built around the Tree House pond, with panels containing information on marshes to familiarize visitors with the forms of life that thrive in wetlands.

◁ *A graceful young girl surrounded by roses in bloom.* The First Jewels, *the work of Romanian artist Alice Winant, was created in New York in 1973.*

Bibliography

Société du Jardin de Chine de Montréal, The Chinese Garden of Montréal, Fides, 1994, 120 p.

Montréal Botanical Garden, Insectarium, Biodome and Planetarium, Les messageries de Presse Benjamin, Inc.,1999, 72 p.

Francine Hoffman, Guide to the Montréal Botanical Garden, Ville de Montréal, 1991, 67 p.

Index

Members of the Québec Gardens' Association

QUEBEC
GARDENS'
ASSOCIATION

1 Mackenzie King Estate

One hundred and sixty miles (200 km) west of Montreal, on the outskirts of Hull, the Mackenzie King Estate was the summer residence of Canada's tenth prime minister for more than half a century. This vast estate (570 acres / 230 ha) includes picturesque ruins, French- and English-style gardens, a rockery, numerous flower gardens, and three restored cottages.

72, chemin Barnes / Chelsea

(819) 827-2020 / Toll free: 1 800 465-1867
www.capcan.ca
Open: mid-May to mid-October
Entrance fee

2 Morgan Arboretum

This magnificent 600 acre (245-hectare) forest reserve, set in the heart of a migratory bird sanctuary at Sainte-Anne-de-Bellevue, showcases a superb collection of native Canadian trees (150 species), including one of the oldest maples on the Island of Montreal. The arboretum is also a great place to spot wildlife. Experimental plantations.

150, chemin des Pins / Sainte-Anne-de-Bellevue

(514) 398-7811
www.total.net/~arbo
Open year-round
Entrance fee

3 Centre de la nature

In Laval, the horticultural capital of Québec, a reclaimed quarry has been turned into the Centre de la nature. This 125-acre (50-hectare) urban park has a lovely collection of ornamental shrubs, native and medicinal plants, annuals, and perennials.

901, avenue Parc / Laval

(450) 662-4942
E-mail: m.latour@ville.laval.qc.ca
Open year-round
No entrance fee

4 Montreal Botanical Gardens

In the heart of Montreal, the Botanical Gardens cover more than 185 acres (75 ha). It features 10 exhibition greenhouses and some 30 outdoor thematic gardens. Its collections originate from all parts of the world. Among its attractions are the Rose Garden (10,000 rose bushes), the Chinese Garden, the Japanese Garden, the Arboretum (100 acres / 40 ha) and its Tree House, and the Insectarium. Guided tours, exhibitions, horticultural workshops, and demonstrations – something for everyone.

4101, rue Sherbrooke Est / Montreal

(514) 872-1400
www.ville.montreal.qc.ca/jardin
Open year-round
Entrance fee

5 The Governor's Garden

This exceptional site in the heart of Old Montreal harbours a rare example of an eighteenth century urban garden. One can find aromatic, medicinal, and decorative plants, as well as fruit trees and a kitchen garden. The Governor's Garden surrounds Château Ramezay Museum, a residence that was built during the French Regime.

Château Ramezay Museum
280, rue Notre-Dame Est / Old Montreal

(514) 861-3708
www.chateauramezay.qc.ca
Open year-round
Entrance fee to the museum only

6 Jardin Daniel A. Séguin

This series of teaching gardens, open to the public for the past five years, is affiliated with the Institut de technologie agroalimentaire. Twelve acres (4.5 ha) are devoted to different themes: a French garden, Japanese and Zen gardens, a water garden, and an old-fashioned Quebec-style garden. Collection of 350 varieties of annuals. Recent additions include 3-D mosaicultures and an ecological vegetable garden. Guided tours included.

3215, rue Sicotte / Saint-Hyacinthe

(450) 778-6504 ext. 215 / In season: (450) 778-0372
www.ita.qc.ca/jardindas
Open: June to September
Entrance fee

7 À Fleur D'eau, floral park

On the vineyard route, the floral park «À Fleur D'eau» displays a variety of aquatic and moisture loving plants. In this natural setting, there are landscaped paths and four lakes, connected by streams and waterfalls. Dedicated to the protection of the aquatic milieu, this park invites you to relax as you explore the calming world of water and a mile-long woodland walk.

140, route 202 / Stanbridge East

(450) 248-7008
E-mail: fleurdo@netc.net
Open: June to October
Entrance fee.

Parc Marie-Victorin

Set in the countryside in the Bois-Francs region, bordering the Rivière Nicolet, this recently developed urban park (30 acres / 12 ha) includes a waterfall garden, a bird garden, a garden of economic plants, and a wetland garden. It is all maintained organically.

385, rue Marie-Victorin / Kingsey Falls

(819) 363-2528 / Toll free: 1 888 753-7272
www.ivic.qc.ca/mv
Open: mid-June to mid-September
Entrance fee.

Domaine Joly-De Lotbinière

Recognized as one of the most beautiful gardens in Quebec, the Domaine Joly-De Lotbinière is a large garden landscaped in the heyday of romanticism, 1851. The site offers an encounter with history and nature, a stroll under century-old trees, an explosion of colours and perfumes, a walk through the forest, an adventure by the St. Lawrence, and much more.

Route de Pointe Platon / Sainte-Croix

(418) 926-2462
www.domainejoly.com
Open: Beginning of May to mid-October
Entrance fee

Jardin Roger-Van den Hende

This 15-acre (6-hectare) teaching garden, attached to Laval University, boasts a collection of 2,000 species and cultivars displayed by botanical family – an arrangement you won't find anywhere else in North America. It includes a water garden, a collection of herbaceous plants and rhododendrons, an arboretum, and a rose garden. Guided tours for groups.

Laval University, Pavillon de l'Envirotron

2480, boulevard Hochelaga / Sainte-Foy
(418) 656-3410
www.ulaval.ca
Open: end of April to late September
No entrance fee

Domaine Maizerets

Owned by the Séminaire de Québec from 1705 to 1979, this largely wooded urban park today covers an area of 67 acres (27 hectares). Visitors can admire the manor house (designated an historic monument), the arboretum, the pond with many aquatic plants, and the various gardens. Artistic and cultural activities.

2000, boulevard Montmorency / Québec

(418) 691-2385 / (418) 691-7842
Open year-round
No entrance fee

 ## National Battlefields Park

This enormous park (268 acres / 108 hectares) was where the French and English armies met in 1759, in one of the most significant military battles in the history of North America. In addition to thousands of trees, visitors can admire many mosaics and the lovely Jeanne-d'Arc garden, a perennial garden in both the French and English styles. Among its themes, the Canada Odyssey exhibition explores the origins of flora and reveals the role played by the Plains of Abraham.

835 Wilfrid-Laurier Avenue / Quebec City

(418) 648-4071
www.ccbn-nbc.gc.ca
Open year-round
Free admission to the park; entrance fee to the exhibit

 ## Henry Stuart House

An enchanting cottage-style garden full of roses surrounds this small house built in 1849. The garden, building, and interior, all unchanged since the 1920s, are designated an historic monument. Thematic exhibitions, concerts.

82, Grande-Allée Ouest / Quebec City

(418) 647-4347 / Toll free: 1 800 494-4347
www.cmsq.qc.ca
Open year-round
Entrance fee

 ## Parc du Bois-de-Coulonge

This magnificent 60-acre (24-hectares) estate was once the residence of Quebec's Lieutenant-Governors. The cliffside English garden overlooking the St. Lawrence features a water garden, borders, roses, and vines, not to mention many different varieties of lilacs, rhododendrons, and azaleas. There are some one hundred species of trees in the woodland park.

1215, chemin Saint-Louis / Sillery

(418) 528-0773 / Toll free:1 800 442-0773
E-mail: commission@capitale.gouv.qc.ca
Open year-round
No entrance fee

 ## Grands Jardins de Normandin

These recently created gardens, covering 135 acres (55 ha), offer visitors a look at the art of gardening throughout the centuries, with their French- and English-style gardens, herb garden, decorative kitchen garden, and Oriental carpet-style garden, featuring 65,000 flowering annual plants in all. Woodland paths.

1515, avenue du Rocher / Normandin

(418) 274-1993 / Toll free: 1 800 920-1993
www.cigp.com/jardin.html
Open: late June to late September
Entrance fee

16   Seigneurie des Aulnaies

Learn about seigniorial life in the last century as you explore this pretty Victorian manor house (1853) and mill (1842). Ornamental garden, kitchen garden, and pinetree wood. Outdoor café, guides in period costume.

525, rue de la Seigneurie / Saint-Roch-des-Aulnaies

(418) 354-2800 / or toll free at 1 877 354-2800
www.laseigneuriedesaulnaies.qc.ca
Open: mid-May to mid-October
Entrance fee

17   Temiscouata Rose Garden (Cabano)

Next to Fort Ingall (1839), on the shores of Lac Temiscouata, this rose garden boasts 1,200 climbing, rambling, bush, and shrub roses representing 250 varieties and species, most of them hardy. Reception garden, classic maze garden, English garden, teaching garden.

81, rue de Caldwell / Cabano
(418) 854-2375
www.roseraie.qc.ca
Open: June to late September
Entrance fee

18   Reford Gardens (Jardins de Métis)

These exceptionally beautiful gardens are nestled at the confluence of the Mitis and St. Lawrence Rivers. With their unique microclimate, the 42 acre (17-ha) gardens are home to 3,000 species and varieties of native and exotic plants. A brook leads visitors past luxurious flowers to the blue poppy glade, for which Reford Gardens are famous. The International Garden Festival is an annual event featuring temporary gardens created by designers from around the world.

200, route 132 / Grand-Metis
(418) 775-2221
www.refordgardens.com
Open: June to mid-October
Entrance fee